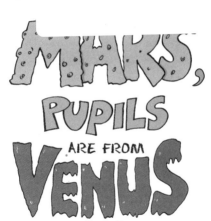

A Red Fox Book

Published by Random House Children's Books
20 Vauxhall Bridge Road, London SW1V 2SA

A division of The Random House Group Ltd
London Melbourne Sydney Auckland
Johannesburg and agencies throughout the world

Text and illustrations © John Byrne 2001

3 5 7 9 10 8 6 4 2

Printed and bound in China

THE RANDOM HOUSE GROUP Limited Reg. No. 954009

ISBN 0 09 940972 0

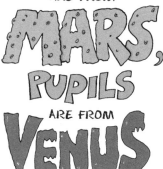

TEACHERS ARE FROM MARS, PUPILS ARE FROM VENUS

JOHN BYRNE

RED
FOX

For Eduka Edufuah
with much love and gratitude

INTRODUCTION

Greetings, earthlings, we come in peace. Well, we have to: we're far too busy fighting with each other to bother about you lot. If you don't see eye-to-eye with your teachers, think about what it's like for us... we've got twice as many eyes as you have! We hope you enjoy our alien jokes, but don't let your earth teachers catch you reading them in the classroom – it might turn them into bigger monsters than we are!

signed **XZZYRLLX**

Alien Pupil

What do alien pupils play
on the chalkboard?
Astronauts and crosses.

ALIEN TEACHER: If I had two apples
in one hand and three apples in my
other hand, what would I have then?
ALIEN PUPIL: Six more hands with
nothing in them!

What newspaper do
alien teachers read?
The News Out of the World.

ALIEN TEACHER: What's the difference between a rocket and a fly?
ALIEN PUPIL: Rockets can fly, but flies can't rocket.

ALIEN PUPIL: Sorry I'm late for school – I was having a dream that I was flying to Earth.
ALIEN TEACHER: How can a dream make you late for school?
ALIEN PUPIL: I had to stop on Venus to ask directions.

How did the moon monster feel
when his teacher was off sick?
He was beaming.

How does the moon monster
teacher punish his pupils?
Eclipse them round the ear.

FIRST ALIEN PUPIL: Our teacher's
got outer space teeth.
SECOND ALIEN PUPIL: What do you
mean 'outer space teeth'?
FIRST ALIEN PUPIL: He's got lots of
big black holes.

Did you hear about the clumsy alien pupil?
He broke the sound barrier.

FIRST ALIEN TEACHER: Who was that pupil I saw you with yesterday called?
SECOND ALIEN TEACHER: Dinner.

Did you hear about the alien pupil who tried to blow up his teacher's spaceship?
He burnt his mouth on the exhaust pipe.

WHY ARE PUPILS WHO TAKE A ROCKET TO SCHOOL ALWAYS LATE?
BECAUSE THEY DON'T COME IN TILL LAUNCH TIME!

ALIEN TEACHER #8

XYRTEROAHR

ALIEN TEACHER #8
Name: XYRTEROAHR

Occupation:
Science Teacher

Description:
This teacher is never short of subject matter - he just gets the class to study him!

Favourite Joke:
Why did the alien science teacher cross the road? He didn't need to - he'd invented a transporter beam to get him across.

Why did the alien dinner lady
yank the tablecloth away?
*She wanted to see some flying
saucers.*

How can you tell if an alien pupil
is rich?
*He comes to school in a
chauffeur-driven flying saucer.*

Why did the alien pupil bite
a chunk out of the sun?
He fancied a light snack.

ALIEN TEACHER: Here's a picture of a typical earthling. How many bones does it have in its body?

ALIEN PUPIL: About 3,000.

ALIEN TEACHER: How did you work that out?

ALIEN PUPIL: He's had a tin of sardines for lunch.

FIRST ALIEN TEACHER: Whenever I leave school, lots of pupils rush to see me off.

SECOND ALIEN TEACHER: I know – they just want to make sure that you're going!

ALIEN PUPIL: I can't seem to get the hang of these earth instruments.
ALIEN MUSIC TEACHER: You mean you haven't managed to play that guitar yet?
ALIEN PUPIL: No, and I've been blowing it all night!

Why did the alien gym teacher buy a pair of water wings?
She was going into deep space.

ALIEN PUPIL: I don't like earthlings.
ALIEN DINNER LADY: Well, just leave them on the side of your plate.

FIRST ALIEN PUPIL: Do our dinner ladies serve rocket meals?
SECOND ALIEN PUPIL: Yes, but they're very hard to keep down.

Where do alien pupils get sent when they are ill?
To the nurse-tronaut.

What do you call an alien pupil's homework?
An unidentified flying project.

OUR TEACHER'S FAVOURITE PLANET IS SATURN...
I'VE NOTICED - MAYBE THAT'S WHY HE SPENDS ALL DAY 'SATURN' HIS BOTTOM DOING NOTHING!

I GOT STUCK IN A TIME WARP AND I'M LATE FOR SCHOOL...
CALM DOWN - LOTS OF PUPILS ARE LATE FOR SCHOOL ...
YES, BUT NOT BY 2,000 YEARS!

What do you find in alien convent schools?
Nun-identified flying objects.

FIRST ALIEN TEACHER: All my pupils like me on first sight.
SECOND ALIEN TEACHER: Yes, it's usually on second sight that they go 'EEEEK!'

How do alien pupils make their school sweatshirt last?
They make their caps and trousers first.

What must an alien pupil do before taking off his schoolbag?
Put on his schoolbag.

FIRST ALIEN PUPIL: I'm late for school – will the next flying saucer be long?
SECOND ALIEN PUPIL: No, it will be round, as usual.

What's green and slimy and has 4,000 legs?
100 forty-legged alien teachers.

ALIEN TEACHER: When do earthlings learn to walk?

ALIEN PUPIL: Er... I don't know.

ALIEN TEACHER: Most earthlings have walked since they were nine months old.

ALIEN PUPIL: Really? They must be very tired.

FIRST SCIENTIST: Do you need any special training for moon rock collecting?

SECOND SCIENTIST: No, you just pick it up as you go along.

WHY COULDN'T THE ALIEN TEACHER STOP HIS PUPILS LARKING ABOUT?
BECAUSE HIS CLASSES HAD NO GRAVITY.

Knock, knock!
Who's there?
Wendy.
Wendy who?
Wendy countdown is over this
rocket can take off.

ALIEN TEACHER: Why do humans
have noses in the middle of their
faces?
ALIEN PUPIL: Because it's
the scenter.

ALIEN TEACHER: What parts of Earth are in outer space?
ALIEN PUPIL: The letters E, A, R and T.

What did the alien pupil bring back from his seaside holiday?
A stick of rocket.

ALIEN TEACHER: A comet is a star with a tail, but can anybody name a famous one?
ALIEN PUPIL: Lassie.

ONE OF OUR ALIEN PUPILS HAS RUN AWAY!
I KNOW - HE'S AN UNIDENTIFIED FLEEING OBJECT!

ALIEN TEACHER #23

RHAORETRYX

ALIEN TEACHER #23
Name: RHAORETRYX

Occupation:
Language Teacher

Description:
None – he tried to describe himself several times to us, but we couldn't understand a word!

Favourite Joke:
Why did the alien language teacher cross the road? *Sorry, The phrase "cross the road" isn't in the Venusian dictionary.*

THERE'S A REALLY STRANGE ALIEN PUPIL IN MY CLASS – INSTEAD OF TWENTY LEGS HE'S ONLY GOT ONE!
TELL HIM TO HOP IT!

The alien teacher and the alien pupil
had an argument about which
of them could jump higher than
the moon. Who was right?
Both of them – the moon can't jump.

What are an alien dinner lady's
three favourite foods?
Men, women, and children.

What do you get when you cross an
alien teacher with a steamroller?
A very flat alien teacher.

Knock, knock!
Who's there?
Jupiter.
Jupiter who?
Jupiter lock on the staff room
door like I told you to?

What has legs like an earthling,
teeth like an earthling, tentacles
like an earthling and is the same
colour as an earthling?
A picture of
an earthling.

ALIEN TEACHER: You pupils had better not mess with me – I can lift an elephant with just one tentacle.

ALIEN PUPIL: Go on, then, prove it.

ALIEN TEACHER: First you've got to find me an elephant with just one tentacle.

How did the alien teacher know his class was full of smelly aliens?
He got a terrible stinking feeling.

What do you get when you cross a parrot with an alien teacher?
A not very pretty Polly.

ALIEN MUSIC TEACHER: Some earthlings can play the piano by ear.
ALIEN PUPIL: Why don't they use their hands like everyone else?

Where do alien teachers cook their breakfast?
In an unidentified frying object.

What do you do when you see an alien teacher?
Hope that the alien teacher hasn't seen you.

I'VE JUST MET AN EARTHLING WHO SAYS MY FACE IS LIKE A FLOWER...
YES MISS – BUT I THINK HE MEANS A CAULIFLOWER!

ALIEN TEACHER #57
Name: YXCRXYZZL

Occupation:
History Teacher

Description:
His classes go on for
5,000,000 light years.
By the time they finish
you are history.

Favourite Joke:
Why did the alien history
teacher cross the road?
That was 5,000,000 light
years ago – how do you
expect me to remember?

ALIEN PUPIL: This earthling painting
is really horrible. What is it called?
ALIEN ART TEACHER: A mirror.

What do you get if you cross ten
alien pupils with Humpty Dumpty?
*Ten green bottoms hanging on
a wall.*

What did the alien pupil say to
the alien dinner lady?
Take me to your larder.

How do you stop an alien teacher
from smelling?
Tie a knot in his nose.

ALIEN TEACHER: Where will you find the biggest aliens in the galaxy?
ALIEN PUPIL: If they're that big, I'm not likely to lose them.

Why couldn't the alien teacher dance?
He had two hundred and fifty left feet.

What do you call an alien teacher with no ears?
Anything you like – she can't hear you.

ALIEN TEACHER: Why are you covering yourself with strawberry jam?

ALIEN PUPIL: To keep space monsters away.

ALIEN TEACHER: But there are no space monsters on this planet.

ALIEN PUPIL: It works then, doesn't it?

ALIEN TEACHER: Why is the letter Y like an alien?

ALIEN PUPIL: Because it's right at the end of the galaxy.

FIRST ALIEN TEACHER: Did you see how I made those alien pupils run?
SECOND ALIEN TEACHER: Yes – they chased you all the way back to your spaceship.

FIRST ALIEN DINNER LADY: How's your appetite?
SECOND ALIEN DINNER LADY: Not good – I haven't eaten anybody in days.

What do you get if you cross a chicken with an alien teacher?
A fowl creature.

Why didn't the alien pupil buy
a new rocket launcher?
Because it cost a bomb.

Why was the alien pupil
sent home from games?
He'd forgotten his tennis rocket.

ALIEN PUPIL: I'd like an earthling
sandwich please.
ALIEN DINNER LADY: I'm sorry,
we couldn't possibly do that.
ALIEN PUPIL: Why? Don't you have
any earthlings?
ALIEN DINNER LADY: Yes – but
we're out of big slices of bread.

WHEN DID THE ALIEN TEACHER FLY TOO CLOSE TO THE SUN?
ARRGH!!
FRY-DAY!!

WHAT ARE YOU BEST AT IN SPACE SCHOOL?
PUTTING AS MUCH SPACE BETWEEN ME AND SCHOOL AS I POSSIBLY CAN!!

FIRST ALIEN TEACHER: Can I interest you in buying this handy calculator?
SECOND ALIEN TEACHER: No thanks – I already know how many hands I've got.

Why did the alien science teacher fill his space station with chewing gum?
He wanted to perform some ex-spearmints.

Why did the alien pupil fill his lunchbox with spaghetti and watches?
Just to pasta time.

ALIEN HEADMASTER: I'm looking for a pupil with one eye called Xzcxxplz.

ALIEN TEACHER: I don't think I know him – but what's the name of his other eye?

ALIEN PUPIL: Give it to me straight, Doc – will I be able to play for the school team after my operation?

ALIEN DOCTOR: Of course you will.

ALIEN PUPIL: Great – they never usually pick me!

What do you get when you cross
an alien teacher with another alien
teacher?
Two very cross alien teachers.

Why did the alien teacher have
a horn on his forehead?
*Because otherwise his lessons
would be pointless.*

FIRST ALIEN PUPIL: Our teacher
thinks she's the steering wheel of
a spaceship.
SECOND ALIEN PUPIL: She needs
to get a grip on herself.

MY TEACHER HATES IT WHEN I TALK IN CLASS...
BUT LOTS OF KIDS TALK IN CLASS.
YES BUT HE WAS TALKING FOR TWO HOURS ON THE TEACHERS SPACE COMMUNICATOR.

FIRST ALIEN PUPIL: What class are you in? First or second year?
SECOND ALIEN PUPIL: Light year.

ALIEN PUPIL: I've got no homework to show you – I had problems storing it on my computer.
ALIEN TEACHER: But it's got a super-powered memory.
FIRST ALIEN: Yes, but I keep forgetting to switch the computer on.

How do alien pupils tie their shoelaces?
With astro-knots.

What's bright orange and looks like an alien teacher?
A bright orange alien teacher.

What's blue and looks like an alien teacher?
A bright orange alien teacher on a very cold day.

What's big and slimy and has red and yellow spots?
A yellow spotted alien with measles.

BUT I'M NOT A MOON MONSTER SIR – I'M FROM PLANET NEPTUNE...
SO HOW COME YOU ONLY COME TO SCHOOL ONCE IN A BLUE MOON?

ALIEN TEACHER #45
Name: LZZYXRCXY

Occupation:
P.E. Teacher

Description:
A nasty alien dictator
who subjects his pupils
to horrible torture.

Favourite Joke:
Why did the alien P.E.
teacher cross the road?
He didn't – he made his
pupils cross the road
200 times instead.

What's pink, lives in outer space
and eats rocks?
A pink rock-eating space monster.

What's pink, lives in outer space
and eats sand?
*A pink rock-eating space monster
on a diet.*

What do you get if you cross an
alien teacher with a dangerous
space monster?
*Very well-behaved
alien pupils.*

Why did the alien put feathers in his spaceship?
He wanted to travel at light speed.

ALIEN PUPIL: I've heard that there's a place on Earth where Friday comes before Thursday.
ALIEN TEACHER: Really, where's that?
ALIEN PUPIL: In the dictionary.

What books do bashful alien pupils read?
Shy-ence fiction.

ALIEN PUPIL: How long were you in teacher training college?
ALIEN TEACHER: Fourteen metres from tentacle to tentacle – the same as I am now!

ALIEN TEACHER: What's the wettest planet in the solar system.
ALIEN PUPIL: U-rain-us.

ALIEN TEACHER: Where are you from?
ALIEN PUPIL: Neptune
ALIEN TEACHER: What part?
ALIEN PUPIL: All of me.

ALIEN PUPIL: Teacher, when we go in the school spaceship, can I put on the radio?
ALIEN TEACHER: No – you'll wear a safety belt like everyone else.

What's green and hairy and goes up and down?
A green hairy alien in a rocket.

ALIEN TEACHER: What do you call a very old spaceship?
ALIEN PUPIL: A dino-saucer.

ALIEN PUPIL: You know, if it wasn't for those purple spots, you'd look just like my sister.

ALIEN TEACHER: But I don't have purple spots.

ALIEN PUPIL: I know, but my sister does.

ALIEN MUM: Why did you put a two-metre-long space snake in your sister's bed?

ALIEN SON: Because I couldn't find a five-metre-long space snake.

T'S MONDAY ORNING - SHOULDN'T ou YOUNG ALIENS E THINKING ABOUT GETTING TO SCHOOL?
WE DON'T MIND THINKING ABOUT IT... IT'S DOING IT WE DON'T LIKE!

ALIEN TEACHER #100

XXVXRZYYXK

ALIEN TEACHER #100
Name: XXVXRZYYXK

Occupation:
Headmaster

Description:
With this many heads
what other job would
you expect him to do?

Favourite Joke:
Why did the alien
headmaster cross the road?
He hasn't yet – he's waiting
for all those heads to finish
looking both ways.

What did the alien teacher say when a witch turned him into a frog?
Nothing – he's never looked better.

DOCTOR: Your face is green, your eyes are red and your tongue is grey!
ALIEN PUPIL: Thank goodness – I was afraid there might be something wrong with me.

How does an alien teacher count to 100?
On her fingers.

ALIEN PUPIL: Teacher, would you shout at me for something I didn't do?

ALIEN TEACHER: Of course not.

ALIEN PUPIL: Good – I didn't do any study last night.

ALIEN PUPIL: Is there intelligent life on Earth?

ALIEN TEACHER: Only when I'm visiting.

ALIEN TEACHER: What do you get if you cross a spaceship with a train?

ALIEN PUPIL: A Choochoo.F.O.

Why was the alien pupil kept home for school?
He was a pale-ien.

ALIEN TEACHER: Which alien was king of the wild frontier?
ALIEN PUPIL: Davy Rocket.

What do aliens write on their holiday postcards?
Wish U.F.O. were here.

Why does the alien caretaker keep the school playing fields so well?
Because he's got green fingers.

ALIEN TEACHER: Can you name ten different aliens you might find in outer space?
ALIEN PUPIL: Yes, sir – a Martian, a Venusian and eight aliens from Saturn.

ALIEN PUPIL: Sir, what's life inside a rocket like?
ALIEN TEACHER: It has its ups and downs.

What kind of spaceship
do sneaky alien pupils drive?
Snoopersonic ones.

ALIEN TEACHER: Why is a meteor like a centre forward?
ALIEN PUPIL: Because it's a shooting star.

ALIEN PUPIL: There's a spaceship in my soup!
ALIEN DINNER LADY: Yes, sir, it's moon-estrone.

What did the dinner ladies say when they were captured by vegetable aliens?
Peas release us.

TO GET ON IN LIFE YOU HAVE TO USE YOUR HEAD...
I KNOW SIR- BUT WHICH HEAD DO YOU MEAN?

DID YOU HEAR ABOUT THE ALIEN PUPIL WHO FLEW A SPACESHIP INTO CLASS?
HE GOT A ROCKET FROM HIS TEACHER!

ALIEN TEACHER: I'm reporting you to the headmaster. Now what's your name?
ALIEN PUPIL: Xarblflymxsynxmzptlnyx.
ALIEN TEACHER: On second thoughts, this time I think I'll let you off with a warning.

FIRST ALIEN PUPIL: Did you hear the joke about the time machine?
SECOND ALIEN PUPIL: It goes in one year and out the other.

What do you say to an alien
teacher with sixteen sets of teeth?
Fangs a lot.

Did you hear about the alien
teacher with two bottoms?
*He believed in chair and
chair alike.*

ALIEN PUPIL: If the school spaceship
turns upside down will we fall out?
ALIEN TEACHER: No – I'll
still speak to you.

How do alien pupils get home from school when they have a cold?
In an Atish-U.F.O.

What do you get if you put a very large alien teacher in a rocket?
A not-very-much-spaceship.

ALIEN PUPIL: When am I going to get served?
ALIEN DINNER LADY: In a minute – I've only got four pairs of hands!

WHAT DO YOU MEAN BY COMING TO SCHOOL COVERED IN CHOCOLATE?
I TOOK A SHORTCUT THROUGH THE MILKY WAY.

What sits in the corner of the
playground and hits itself on
the head with a hammer?
A nail-ien.

What do moon monsters wear
when they cycle to school?
Their bicycle eclipse.

Why are alien teachers
good at art?
*Because all their drawings
are Mars-terpieces.*

Why was no one scared of the
six-legged alien teacher?
Because he was armless.

What was the six-legged alien
teacher's favourite sport?
Foot-foot-foot-foot-foot-football.

What do pupils who misbehave
in space school end up as?
Jail-iens.

What do alien teachers drink in
the staff room?
Gravi-tea.

I'M REALLY LOOKING FORWARD TO THE SCHOOL CAROL CONCERT...
ARE WE HAVING MINCE PIES AFTERWARDS?
NO - WE'RE JUST GOING TO EAT CAROL!

ALIEN PUPIL #103

YXCHRSTTYX

ALIEN PUPIL #103
Name: YXCHRSTTYX

Occupation:
School Swot

Description:
This alien has the largest brain in the galaxy.

Favourite Joke:
Why did the school swot cross the road?
He didn't – his brain's much to heavy for him to actually move.

What do alien dinner ladies keep in the freezer?
Meat-eors.

Where do alien pupils keep their sandwiches?
In their launch boxes.

What do you call a rocket full of school swots?
A tube of smarties.

ALIEN TEACHER: What do you call an alien with a super-powered memory?
ALIEN PUPIL: I forget.

What do you call an alien
pupil with 3,000 arms?
Andy.

What do you call a Martian on
Venus?
Lost.

FIRST ALIEN PUPIL: Is this school
spaceship running on time?
SECOND ALIEN PUPIL: No, it's
running on petrol.

What has six arms and two wheels?
An alien on a bicycle.

What do you call a clumsy alien pupil?
A disastronaut.

Why did the alien teacher bring a donkey into class?
She wanted to teach ass-tronomy.

What's the second slowest thing in the galaxy?
A snail-ien.

What's the slowest thing in the galaxy?
An alien pupil on his way to school.

What's the second fastest thing in the galaxy?
An alien pupil on his way home from school.

What's the fastest thing in the galaxy?
An alien teacher chasing the alien pupil – it wasn't time to go home yet.

ALIEN TEACHER: Why have you got two dogs in your spaceship?
ALIEN PUPIL: I wanted to go pup, pup and away.

Knock, knock!
Who's there?
Orbit.
Orbit who?
Orbit earlier on I got locked out of the classroom.

Why do alien pupils from Saturn mess up the school showers?
They always leave rings.

What planet do most alien dinner ladies come from?
Mer-curry.

MAYBE WE SHOULDN'T HAVE BROUGHT AN ALIEN GOLDEN DELICIOUS APPLE FOR TEACHER...
YEAH- THE APPLE WAS GOLDEN AND TEACHER WAS DELICIOUS...

XYXTTSRHCXY

ALIEN PUPIL #301
Name: XYXTTSRHCXY

Occupation:
School Bully

Description:
The most handsome alien
in the entire universe
(we have to say that
or he'll thump us).

Favourite Joke:
Why did the school
bully cross the road?
He didn't – he made
some smaller aliens
carry him over.

TEACHER SAYS WE - SHOULDN'T FRIGHTEN SMALLER CREATURES..
TROUBLE IS, WHEN YOU'RE A GIANT JELLYMONSTER FROM JUPITER EVERYONE IS A SMALLER CREATURE!

How do alien pupils watch TV?
Through their telly-scopes.

What do you call an alien gym
teacher with feet shaped like stars?
Twinkle toes.

When do alien teachers get their
feet stuck together?
Once in a glue moon.

What's the quickest way to spot
an alien pupil?
Give it chickenpox.

What do moon monsters sing whenever their school team scores a goal?

Here we glow, here we glow, here we glow!

Why do alien teachers have bad breath?

It takes a long time to brush 1,578,246 teeth.

Why don't alien teachers know they have bad breath?

Would YOU tell someone who had 1,578,246 teeth?

What did the school nurse give the alien teacher to cure its bad breath?
An Apollo mint.

Why did the alien geography teacher have Planet Earth painted on her glasses?
Because she wanted to see the world.

ALIEN TEACHER: What do you call a kangaroo with an alien in her pouch?
ALIEN PUPIL: A Mars-upial.

Why did the alien teacher fill his spaceship with metal fasteners?
He wanted to give it a bit more zip.

What do alien dinner ladies put on their christmas cake?
Star-zipan.

ALIEN TEACHER: Why have you climbed into that spaceship's petrol tank?
ALIEN PUPIL: I like making a fuel of myself.

DAD - HOW COME WE POLKA DOT PEOPLE FROM PLUTO NEVER CHEAT AT EXAMS?
BECAUSE WE'RE ALWAYS SPOTTED.

WHY DO YOU KIDS KEEP SWINGING ON MY LEGS LIKE THAT?
'COS WE'RE PLAYING STAR-ZAN!

What do you call an alien with three eyes?
An aliiien.

What is the alien pupil's favourite subject at school?
Arts and spacecrafts.

ALIEN TEACHER: What's grey, craggy and zooms around the Mediterranean Sea?
ALIEN PUPIL: The Rocket of Gibraltar.

Why did the alien pupil wear purple trousers?
They matched his purple hair.

ALIEN TEACHER: Where would you catch the space train?
ALIEN PUPIL: At the space station.

What did the triangular alien say to the square alien?
I haven't seen you around for ages.

What's white and fluffy and found in alien sweet shops?
A Mars mallow.

Why did the alien pupil fill his spaceship with jelly and custard?
He wanted to make it go a trifle faster.

ALIEN TEACHER: Why do earthlings buy birdseed?
ALIEN PUPIL: Maybe they want to grow some birds?

What did the giant alien pupil say to the midget alien pupil?
Let's play squash.

MAKE A WISH ON THAT STAR AND YOU CAN TELL THE WHOLE CLASS IF IT COMES TRUE...
IF IT CAME TRUE I WOULDN'T HAVE TO BE IN CLASS!

FIRST ALIEN PUPIL: Have you heard the joke about the time machine?
SECOND ALIEN PUPIL: No – but someone's going to tell me tomorrow.

Why do 1,000-eyed aliens make good teachers?
They're used to controlling lots of pupils.

What do you call two alien physics teachers having a fight?
Science friction.

FIRST ALIEN TEACHER: I looked out of my rocket window the other day and saw a tortoise flying past.
SECOND ALIEN TEACHER: What would a tortoise be doing in outer space?
FIRST ALIEN TEACHER: About two miles per hour.

Which part of the alien gym teacher's foot was shaped like a planet?
His Plu-toe.

I'VE JUST CAUGHT ONE OF MY PUPILS CHEATING IN THE HISTORY EXAM!
SERVES YOU RIGHT FOR LETTING HIM SNEAK A TIME MACHINE IN UNDER HIS JACKET!

ALIEN PUPIL #75
Name: KYXYYXLL

Occupation:
School Joker

Description:
This alien sits at the back of the class pulling funny faces.

Favourite Joke:
Why did the school joker cross the road? He was chased across by a gang of aliens who were sick of their funny faces being pulled.

I CAN'T DO GAMES TODAY – I'VE COME OUT IN PURPLE SPOTS!
THAT'S AWFUL! YOU'RE SUPPOSED TO BE COVERED IN BLUE SPOTS!

ALIEN TEACHER: Which is the world's largest sea?
ALIEN PUPIL: The galax-sea.

ALIEN TEACHER: What's that spaceship doing on the stairs?
ALIEN PUPIL: Someone must have left the landing light on.

What do you call a very old alien teacher?
A grey-lien.

FIRST ALIEN PUPIL: Our teacher's on a new diet.
SECOND ALIEN PUPIL: I know – she only eats earthlings who are under 300 calories.

Why did the alien dinner lady put a spaceship in her dishwasher?
She wanted to go for a spin.

Why didn't the alien music teacher need an instrument?
She already had her own horns.

Why did the alien pupil put a frog in his spaceship?
He only wanted to go for a short hop.

ALIEN TEACHER: Where would you find Venusian cows?
ALIEN PUPIL: In a science fiction moo-vie.

Why was the alien pupil playing football in his flying saucer?
He was practising for the cup.

ALIEN TEACHER: Shall I read you War of the Worlds?

ALIEN PUPIL: Is that the novel where Earth is saved from an invasion?

ALIEN TEACHER: That's right.

ALIEN PUPIL: No thanks – I prefer stories with happy endings.

Why is it expensive to go to space school?

Because the fees are astronomical.

Why should a sick alien be kept home from school?

In case he takes Saturn for the worse.

I HEAR YOUR NEW MUSIC TEACHER IS ONE OF THE STONE MEN FROM SATURN...
YES AND ALL HE EVER PLAYS IS ROCK MUSIC!

ALIEN PUPIL #54

LLXYYXYK

ALIEN PUPIL #54
Name: LLXYYXYK

Occupation:
Teacher's Pet

Description:
This alien is kept in a cage
at the back of the class.

Favourite Joke:
Why did the teacher's
pet cross the road?
He crossed the road!
Oh no! He's escaped
from the cage!

HEADMASTER I'M HAVING BIG PROBLEMS WITH MY INVISIBLE ALIEN PUPILS!
TELL THEM I WANT TO NOT SEE THEM AFTER CLASS!

FIRST ALIEN PUPIL: What did Sir do before he became a teacher?

SECOND ALIEN PUPIL: He ran a rocket factory, but it closed down.

FIRST ALIEN PUPIL: Why did it do that?

SECOND ALIEN PUPIL: He could never get his business off the ground.

What is the alien teacher's favourite part of the newspaper? *The star signs.*

What does Father Christmas say
when he visits alien pupils?
U.F.Hohoho.

What flowers grow on the other side
of the moon?
Sun flowers.

What did one lump of space rock
say to the other lump of space rock?
Meteor at the corner after school?

What kind of poetry do they study
in alien English class?
Uni-verse.

FIRST ALIEN PUPIL: I do wish I didn't have a green spotty nose.
SECOND ALIEN PUPIL: Count yourself lucky! Aliens from my planet don't even have noses.
FIRST ALIEN PUPIL: Then how do you smell?
SECOND ALIEN PUPIL: A lot nicer than you do!

What's the last thing an alien teacher does before leaving the classroom?
He switches off the satel-lite.

ALIEN PUPIL: There's a fly in my soup.
ALIEN DINNER LADY: I'm sorry. I'll bring you a new bowl immediately.
ALIEN PUPIL: I should think so – when I order fly soup, I expect to find a lot more than just one fly in there!

ALIEN PUPIL: I'm a space monster!
ALIEN TEACHER: You certainly are – you've got a lot of space between your ears!

SOMEBODY IN MY CLASS IS MAKING UP STORIES ABOUT ME BUT I DON'T KNOW WHO IT IS...
MUST BE AN UNIDENTIFIED LYING OBJECT!

OH NO! I FORGOT TO HAVE MY SCHOOL PHOTO TAKEN! MUM WILL KILL ME!
NO SHE WON'T - GIVE HER THIS PICTURE OF MY SET OF BAGPIPES - SHE'LL NEVER KNOW THE DIFFERENC

What shampoo do moon monsters
use after football practice?
Wash and glow.

FIRST ALIEN PUPIL: We locked
our teacher inside a rocket!
SECOND ALIEN PUPIL: How did
he feel about that?
FIRST ALIEN PUPIL: He was over
the moon.

Why did the alien pupil bring
an apple to school?
*Because he wanted to be
creature's pet.*

Which planet has the hardest working alien dinner ladies?
Chew-piter.

An alien teacher had fifteen hands – which one did she use to write on the chalkboard?
She didn't – she used chalk.

Did you hear about the short-sighted alien teacher?
She went for an eye,
eye, eye, eye,
eye test.

Why did the alien teacher have green spots all over her body? *Because if she had purple ones she'd look silly.*

SCHOOL NURSE: Can you read the bottom line of my chart?
ALIEN PUPIL: Sure – it says XYLMPZXIPZ.
SCHOOL NURSE: Gosh! How did you get that right so quickly?
ALIEN PUPIL: It is the name of my next-door neighbour.

Why did the alien teacher leave his wristwatch in his rocket?
He wanted to make time fly.

How many alien teachers does it take to launch a rocket?
5 ... 4 ... 3 ... 2 ... 1!

How do alien pupils play badminton?
With a space shuttle.

Why did the alien dinner lady paint her spaceship bright red?
She wanted a tomato saucer.

What do you call an alien who gets expelled from school?
An Unidentified Flying Reject.

Why did the alien dinner lady want a tomato saucer?
So no other ship could ketchup.

Why is it easy to fool an aiien teacher?
Because he has 2,450 legs to pull.

Which planet do alien music teachers come from?
Nep-tune.

HAVE YOU EVER GONE INTO AN EXAM WITH THE ANSWERS WRITTEN UP YOUR SLEEVE?
OF COURSE NOT- WITH THIS MANY ARMS I CAN HAVE THE ENTIRE BOOK WRITTEN UP MY SLEEVE!

ALIEN PUPIL #32

GEORGE

ALIEN PUPIL #32
Name: GEORGE

Occupation:
Exchange Student from Earth

Description:
URGH! This creature is so ugly we aliens just can't look at him, let alone describe him.

Favourite Joke:
We don't know – every time we ask him about crossing the road, he starts banging on about some earth creature called a chicken.

What is the alien pupil's favourite soft drink?
Lemon and slime.

ALIEN PUPIL: I keep thinking I'm a moon!
SCHOOL NURSE: What's come over you?
ALIEN PUPIL: So far several cows and a cat with a fiddle.

WHY DO YOU ALIEN PUPILS KEEP GLOWING IN CLASS?
BECAUSE YOUR LESSONS LEAVE US IN THE DARK!

Why are there no vampires in outer space?
Because of the garlic-sea.

What did the alien with sixty legs say when he met an alien with seventy arms?
Gosh – that's handy.

Why did the alien pupil only pay attention in time travel class?
So he could enjoy Teachers Are From Mars, Pupils Are From Venus *all over again.*